# FUN PUZZLE CHALLENGES™

# MENSA for kids:

# FUN PUZZLE CHALLENGES™

## TERRIFIC WAYS
## To Stretch Your
## BRAIN!

### EVELYN B. CHRISTENSEN

Sky Pony Press
New York

*This book is dedicated to my wonderful family and to a loving God, who is the ultimate problem solver.*

—*Evelyn*

Sky Pony Press books may be purchased in bulk at special discounts for sales promotion, corporate gifts, fund-raising, or educational purposes. Special editions can also be created to specifications. For details, contact the Special Sales Department, Sky Pony Press, 307 West 36th Street, 11th Floor, New York, NY 10018 or info@skyhorsepublishing.com.

Sky Pony® is a registered trademark of Skyhorse Publishing, Inc.®, a Delaware corporation.

Visit our website at www.skyponypress.com.

10 9 8 7 6 5 4

This product conforms to CPSIA 2008

Library of Congress Cataloging-in-Publication Data is available on file.

Cover design by Mona Lin

Print ISBN: 978-1-5107-3861-4

Printed in China

# Contents

# Puzzles

# 1. Fill-In Fun Addition

Pick a top number and a side number. Where their column and row meet is the sum. Fill in the blank squares.

| + | | |
|---|---|---|
| | 8 | 12 |
| 2 | | |
| 6 | 9 | |

| + | | 8 | |
|---|---|---|---|
| | 6 | | 8 |
| | 5 | 11 | |
| | | | 13 |

# 2. Addition Squares

Find the missing numbers. In each row, the fourth number is the sum of the first three. The same is true of each column.

(A)

| 2 |    |    | 13 |
|----|----|----|----|
|    |    | 6  | 9  |
| 1  | 8  |    |    |
|    | 12 | 18 | 36 |

(B)

|    | 1  | 3  |    |
|----|----|----|----|
| 3  |    | 1  | 8  |
|    | 6  |    | 11 |
| 12 |    | 9  |    |

# 3. Snowman Logic

Cal, Ling, Mirka, and Will each built a snowman, and each gave their snowman different headgear: a top hat, a cowboy hat, a baseball cap, and a cooking pot. Use the clues to decide who used which item on their snowman.

1. What Cal used starts with the same letter as his name.
2. Mirka told the person using the top hat that he should tilt it more.
3. Ling said she bought the hat she used at a rodeo.

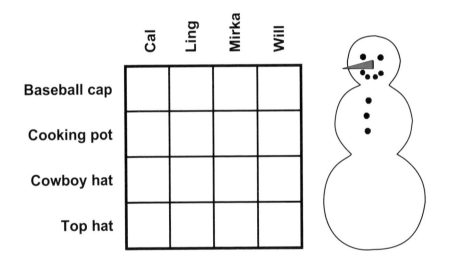

Use the grid to eliminate possibilities. Put an "x" in a box if a "hat" doesn't go with a person. Put an "o" if it does.

# 4. Word Wrappers

For each blank use two or more of the letters in the underlined word to make a new word that will logically fit in the sentence. The letters in your new word must be in the same order as in the underlined word.

1. The <u>bears</u> will _____ removed from behind the _____ and set free.

2. The _____ stood by the flag _____ as he spoke to the <u>people</u>.

3. _____ can _____ help _____ with my <u>homework</u>?

4. If _____ a tree falls on her drive, the <u>clever</u> woman will use a _____ to move it.

5. Dad let out a _____ at the <u>sight</u> of my bloody knee, then had me _____ while he bandaged _____.

6. It will take strong <u>effort</u> _____ luck _____ us to save the _____.

7. We had to <u>plead</u> with the native _____ to _____ us through the jungle.

8. In the _____ afternoon, we _____ on the <u>slate</u> rock and _____ our snack.

# 5. Tangled Strings

Match the kites with their owners.

**Alexandra    Carly    Eliza    Georgina    Tyler**

Extra challenge: use only your eyes to follow the strings.

# 6. Fill-In Fun Addition

Pick a top number and a side number. Where their column and row meet is the sum. Fill in the blank squares.

|  + |    |  9 |
|----|----|----|
|    | 29 |    |
|    |    | 23 |
|  8 | 25 |    |

|  + | 15 |    |    |
|----|----|----|----|
| 18 |    | 25 | 34 |
|    | 24 |    |    |
|    |    |    | 29 |

# 7. Venn Puzzler

Ms. Readalot, the librarian, is hosting a reading celebration sleepover. She has ordered 24 pizzas. Use the Venn diagram to help you find the answers to the questions below.

- 10 pizzas have mushrooms.
- 11 pizzas have pepperoni.
- 8 pizzas are cheese only, with no toppings.

How many pizzas have only mushrooms? _____
How many pizzas have only pepperoni? _____
How many pizzas have both mushrooms and pepperoni?_____

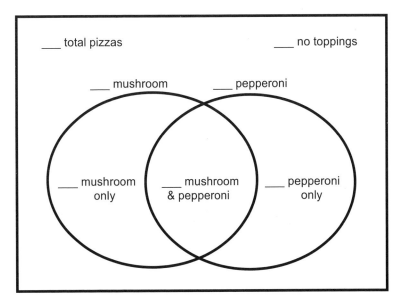

# 8. Addition Squares

Find the missing numbers. In each row, the fourth number is the sum of the first three. The same is true of each column.

**A**

| | 4 | | 15 |
|---|---|---|---|
| 2 | | 6 | |
| 5 | | | 12 |
| 14 | | 11 | 38 |

**B**

| 1 | | 2 | |
|---|---|---|---|
| 3 | 8 | | 15 |
| | | 7 | 16 |
| 13 | 14 | | |

# 9. Space Word Scramble

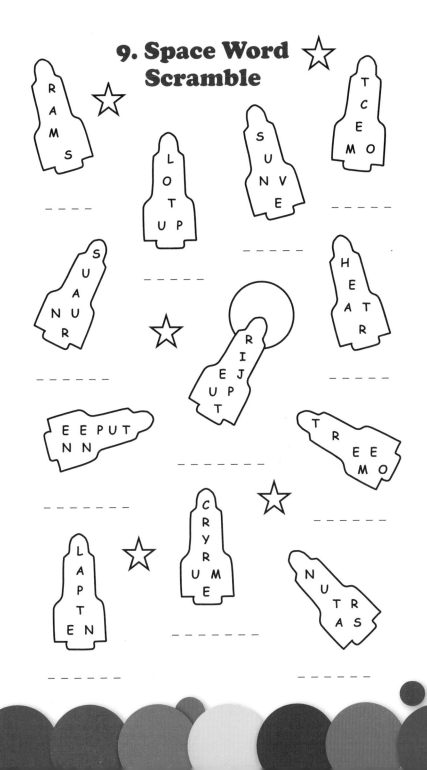

# 10. Word Builder for CASTLE

How many words, 3 letters or longer, can you spell using just the letters in the word "**CASTLE**"? Plurals are allowed but no abbreviations, proper nouns, or foreign words.

_____   _____   _____

_____   _____   _____

_____   _____   _____

_____   _____   _____

_____   _____   _____

_____   _____   _____

_____   _____   _____

_____   _____   _____

_____   _____   _____

_____   _____

_____   _____

_____   _____

_____   _____

10—Good start!   20—Excellent!   30 or more—Outstanding!

# 11. Division Sudoku

Solve the problems. Then fill in the squares so that each row, column, and 2 x 3 rectangle has the numbers 4–9.

| | 35 ÷ 7 | | | 48 ÷ 6 | |
|---|---|---|---|---|---|
| 32 ÷ 4 | | | 54 ÷ 9 | 28 ÷ 7 | |
| 30 ÷ 6 | | 16 ÷ 4 | | | 49 ÷ 7 |
| | 24 ÷ 3 | | 63 ÷ 7 | | 36 ÷ 9 |
| 72 ÷ 8 | 42 ÷ 7 | | | 56 ÷ 8 | |
| | | | 45 ÷ 9 | | 36 ÷ 6 |

# 12. Fill-In Fun Multiplication

Pick a top number and a side number. Where their column and row meet is the product. Fill in the blank squares.

| X | 2 | |
|---|---|---|
| | 12 | |
| 3 | | 18 |
| | | 24 |

| X | | 3 | |
|---|---|---|---|
| | | 24 | |
| 4 | 36 | | 24 |
| | 18 | | |

# 13. MENSA Wordoku

Fill in the squares so that each row, column, and 5-square section has the letters M-E-N-S-A.

| | S | | | |
|---|---|---|---|---|
| | | | N | |
| E | | S | M | |
| | E | | | A |
| | | A | | M |

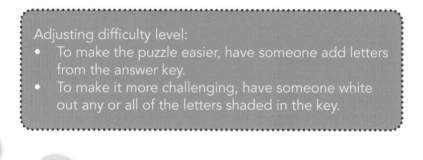

Adjusting difficulty level:
- To make the puzzle easier, have someone add letters from the answer key.
- To make it more challenging, have someone white out any or all of the letters shaded in the key.

# 14. Clues for Climbing

Meg, John, Sarah, and Zeke all like to climb trees, but they each have a different favorite kind. Use the clues to decide who likes which kind of tree best: apple, maple, oak, or pear.

1.  Zeke's favorite is not a fruit tree.
2.  One of the kids enjoys watching squirrels gather acorns from her favorite tree.
3.  The fruit Sarah ate from her favorite tree was not a pear.

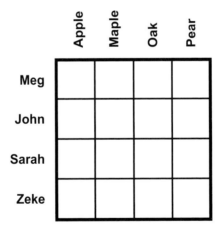

|       | Apple | Maple | Oak | Pear |
|-------|-------|-------|-----|------|
| Meg   |       |       |     |      |
| John  |       |       |     |      |
| Sarah |       |       |     |      |
| Zeke  |       |       |     |      |

Use the grid to eliminate possibilities. Put an "x" in a box if a tree doesn't go with a person. Put an "o" if it does.

# 15. Clip Clue Math Puzzles

Use the clues to put the clips in the correct order. The number below a clip indicates its value.

**PUZZLE A**

**Use 2 blue clips, 1 green clip, and 1 red clip.**

**CLUE 1:**  The red clip is worth twice a blue clip.
**CLUE 2:**  A blue clip is worth twice the red clip.

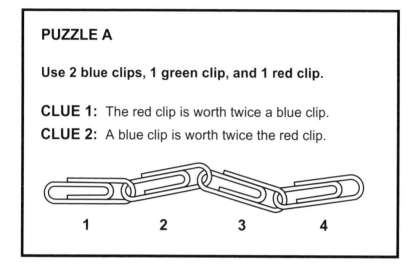

**PUZZLE B**

**Use a blue clip, green clip, red clip, and yellow clip.**

**CLUE 1:**  The green clip comes before the blue clip.
**CLUE 2:**  The sum of the blue and yellow clips
equals another clip.

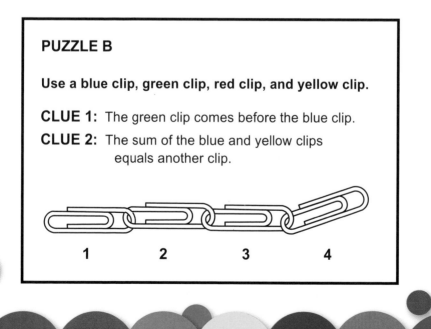

# 16. Fill-In Fun Multiplication

Pick a top number and a side number. Where their column and row meet is the product. Fill in the blank squares.

| X |    |    |
|---|----|----|
|   |    | 20 |
| 8 |    | 32 |
| 7 | 56 |    |

| X |    |    |    |
|---|----|----|----|
| 6 |    | 18 | 54 |
|   | 63 |    |    |
|   | 35 | 15 |    |

# 17. Monster Mix-Up

The monsters in each row, column, and the two main diagonals have something that's the same for them, but is different from the other six monsters. Can you figure out what?

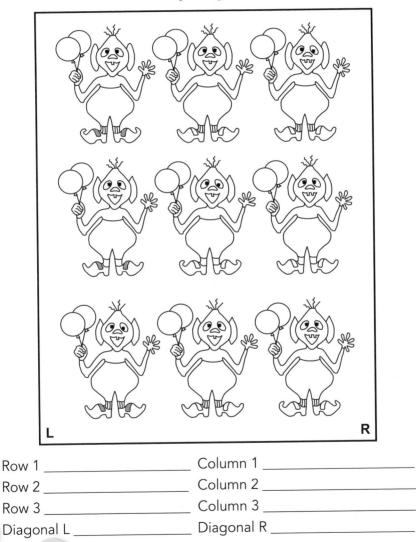

Row 1 _____   Column 1 _____

Row 2 _____   Column 2 _____

Row 3 _____   Column 3 _____

Diagonal L _____   Diagonal R _____

# 18. TSUNAMI Wordoku

A tsunami is a really large ocean wave. Fill in the squares so that each row, column, and 7-square section has the letters T-S-U-N-A-M-I.

| | N | | I | U | | M |
|---|---|---|---|---|---|---|
| U | | | | N | S | T |
| T | | | M | | U | A |
| M | A | | | I | | |
| | | M | S | T | A | |
| I | S | U | | | | N |
| | | S | N | | I | |

Adjusting difficulty level:
- To make the puzzle easier, have someone add letters from the answer key.
- To make it more challenging, have someone white out any or all of the letters shaded in the key.

# 19. Word Wrappers

For each blank use two or more of the letters in the underlined word to make a new word that will logically fit in the sentence. The letters in your new word must be in the same order as in the underlined word.

1. Grandpa asked _____ to _____ the _____ on the weeds behind the <u>house</u>.

2. Isabel needs to _____ _____ tablecloth that has <u>hermit</u> crabs embroidered on _____.

3. _____ will _____ a _____ fee _____ the <u>flowers</u> if we order online.

4. Please _____ the <u>gelatin</u> _____ the _____ pan from the refrigerator.

5. Will you _____ for _____ of the _____ showcased _____ the <u>party</u>?

6. _____ took the statistics as an _____ that <u>women</u> had _____ some progress in matching the salaries of _____.

7. This _____ _____ _____ to be a welcome <u>surprise</u> at the dinner.

8. The _____ shoveled the <u>manure</u> from the stall of the _____ with the long _____.

# 20. Fishing for Answers

A group of friends went fishing together. Anna, Chloe, Felix, Juan, and Miguel each caught one fish. The fish were each a different length: 4", 5", 7", 8", and 10". Use the clues to decide who caught which fish.

1.  Chloe's fish was half as long as Anna's fish.
2.  Miguel's fish was 2" longer than Juan's fish.
3.  Anna did not catch the longest fish.

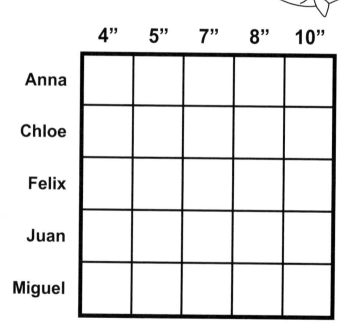

|        | 4" | 5" | 7" | 8" | 10" |
|--------|----|----|----|----|-----|
| Anna   |    |    |    |    |     |
| Chloe  |    |    |    |    |     |
| Felix  |    |    |    |    |     |
| Juan   |    |    |    |    |     |
| Miguel |    |    |    |    |     |

Use the grid to eliminate possibilities. Put an "x" in a box if a length doesn't go with a person. Put an "o" if it does.

# 21. Insect Word Scramble

K I   T E
  C
R     C

_(_) _ _ _ _ _

  S     F
    E
  L     I

_ _ (_) _

O H M T

_ _ _ _

E       B
  E L
  E     T

_ _ _ _ _ _

L E A F

_ _ _ _

  C     R
    A
  O     H

_ _ _ (_)

P A W S

_ (_) _

G L   U B
    A
  D     Y

_ _ (_) _ _ _

C I E L

_ _ _ _

  C     T
    O S
  U     L

_ _ _ _ _ _

  P     D
    A
  I     H

(_) _ _ _

T I   M E
    E
R       T

_ _ _ _ _ _ _

Use the circled letters to spell another insect: _ _ _ _ _ _

# 22. Slippery Slopes

Fill in numbers, operation signs, or both, so that starting with the number in the top circle, then doing each operation as you come to it, brings you to the number in the last circle. Use only positive whole numbers.

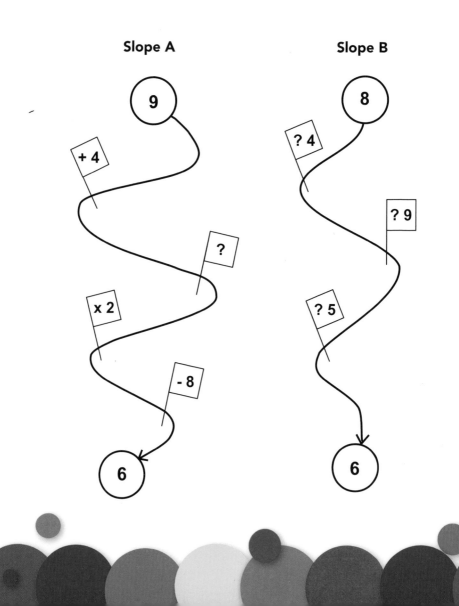

# 23. Animal Word Search

| W | A | L | R | U | S | R | A |
|---|---|---|---|---|---|---|---|
| A | C | A | T | P | U | E | L |
| S | A | W | I | M | A | G | A |
| H | M | D | E | E | R | I | O |
| A | E | L | T | R | U | T | K |
| R | L | E | L | A | H | W | U |
| K | E | D | I | U | Q | S | A |
| B | E | A | R | B | A | R | C |

Words go right, left, up, down, and diagonally.

| AUK | BEAR | LEMUR | SPIDER |
|-----|------|-------|--------|
| BEE | CRAB | SHARK | TURTLE |
| CAT | CAMEL | SHREW | WALRUS |
| EEL | KOALA | WHALE | |
| EMU | SQUID | | |
| DEER | TIGER | | |

# 24. Detective Eyes

Find the two squares that have the symbols in exactly the same positions.

| | | | |
|---|---|---|---|
| Ψ Ω<br>Λ ♥ | ♥ Ω<br>Λ Ψ | Λ ♥<br>Ω Ψ | Ω Ψ<br>Λ ♥ |
| ♥ Ψ<br>Λ Ω | Ω Λ<br>♥ Ψ | Ψ ♥<br>Ω Λ | Λ Ω<br>♥ Ψ |
| Ω Ψ<br>Λ ♥ | Ψ ♥<br>Λ Ω | Λ ♥<br>Ψ Ω | Ψ Λ<br>Ω ♥ |
| ♥ Ω<br>Ψ Λ | Ω Ψ<br>♥ Λ | Ω Λ<br>Ψ ♥ | Λ Ω<br>Ψ ♥ |
| Ω ♥<br>Ψ Λ | Ψ Λ<br>♥ Ω | Ψ Ω<br>♥ Λ | ♥ Ψ<br>Ω Λ |

# 25. TOUCAN Wordoku

A toucan is a colorful tropical bird with a really big beak. Fill in the squares so that each row, column, and 6-square section has the letters T-O-U-C-A-N.

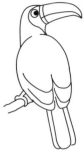

|   |   | O | C |   | N |
|---|---|---|---|---|---|
| O |   | C |   | T |   |
|   | N |   |   |   |   |
|   |   | A |   | N | U |
| A | T |   |   |   | O |
|   |   | U |   | A |   |

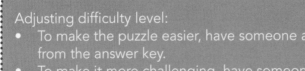

Adjusting difficulty level:
- To make the puzzle easier, have someone add letters from the answer key.
- To make it more challenging, have someone white out any or all of the letters shaded in the key.

# 26. Coin Clue Puzzles

Using pennies, nickels, dimes, or quarters, put the coins in the correct order according to the clues.

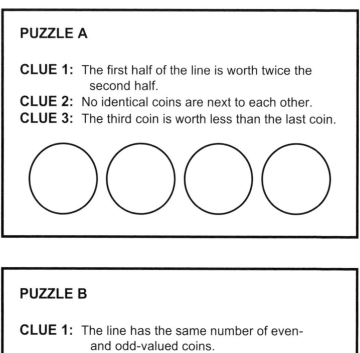

**PUZZLE A**

**CLUE 1:** The first half of the line is worth twice the second half.
**CLUE 2:** No identical coins are next to each other.
**CLUE 3:** The third coin is worth less than the last coin.

**PUZZLE B**

**CLUE 1:** The line has the same number of even- and odd-valued coins.
**CLUE 2:** The sum of the first two coins is worth 4¢ less than the last coin.
**CLUE 3:** The second coin is not brown.

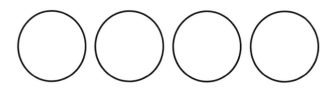

# 27. Word Builder for TALENTS

How many words, 3 letters or longer, can you spell using just the letters in the word "**TALENTS**"? Abbreviations, proper nouns, and foreign words are not allowed.

| | | |
|---|---|---|
| _____ | _____ | _____ |
| _____ | _____ | _____ |
| _____ | _____ | _____ |
| _____ | _____ | _____ |
| _____ | _____ | _____ |
| _____ | _____ | _____ |
| _____ | _____ | _____ |
| _____ | _____ | _____ |
| _____ | _____ | _____ |
| _____ | _____ | _____ |
| _____ | _____ | _____ |
| _____ | _____ | _____ |
| _____ | _____ | _____ |

10—Good start!   25—Excellent!   40 or more—Outstanding!

# 28. Word Wrappers

For each blank use two or more of the letters in the
underlined word to make a new word that will logically fit
in the sentence. The letters in your new word must be in
the same order as in the underlined word.

1.  In the fairy _____, the baby was _____ to lift a heavy
    <u>table</u>.

2.  Bells will _____ and rose <u>petals</u> will be tossed when the
    princess and her _____ get their new _____.

3.  _____ <u>notice</u> was posted to inform us the _____
    machine was _____ working.

4.  The new _____ _____ in her parents' _____, but
    was quick to <u>scamper</u> off when they got to _____.

5.  She will <u>educate</u> her _____ on what her _____ will
    want to _____ when he cares for her pet.

6.  Usually it is _____ for him to _____ with his bad
    _____, but that time _____ _____ <u>heard</u> just fine.

7.  Please _____ to <u>return</u> this antique _____ to the
    customer who left it behind.

8.  The clown wearing silly _____ and a _____ _____
    me _____ on the <u>elephants</u> and _____ them.

# 29. Venn Puzzler

The fifth graders gathered bags of paper, plastic, and glass to recycle. Glass had to be separate from paper and plastic. Use the given information and the Venn diagram to help you answers the questions.

- 13 bags had paper.
- 8 bags had both paper and plastic.
- Twice as many bags had plastic as had just paper.
- There was 1 more bag with glass than with just plastic.

How many more bags had just paper than had just plastic? _____
How many total bags of recyclables did the fifth graders collect? _____

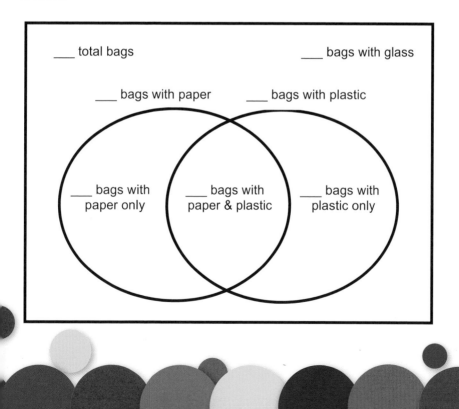

___ total bags                          ___ bags with glass

___ bags with paper        ___ bags with plastic

___ bags with          ___ bags with          ___ bags with
paper only          paper & plastic          plastic only

# 30. Rhyme-It with SIGH

Many words rhyme with "SIGH." Below are clues for 30 of them. How many can you name and spell correctly?

1. _ _ _ not wet
2. _ _ _ a dessert
3. _ _ _ weep
4. _ _ _ _ not low
5. _ _ _ purchase
6. _ _ _ pig's home
7. _ _ _ stop living
8. _ _ _ seeing organ
9. _ _ _ soar
10. _ _ _ untruth
11. _ _ _ change the color
12. _ _ _ where the sun is
13. _ _ _ a grain
14. _ _ _ cook in oil
15. _ _ _ secret agent

16. _ _ _ fellow
17. _ _ _ bashful
18. _ _ _ bind
19. _ _ _ question word
20. _ _ _ force open
21. _ _ _ sneaky
22. _ _ _ farewell word
23. _ _ _ _ contradict
24. _ _ _ _ agile, lively
25. _ _ _ _ _ answer
26. _ _ _ _ _ _ upper leg
27. _ _ _ attempt
28. _ _ _ _ supporter
29. _ _ _ _ depend on
30. _ _ _ _ _ _ _ night song

# 31. Which Design Is Unique?

Three of these designs are the same, but one is different.
Find the unique one.

**A.**

**B.**

**C.**

**D.**

# 32. A Puzzle about Puzzles

Paul and Katie love puzzles! Last month they worked five different kinds, a different number of each kind. Use the clues to decide how many of each kind.

1. They worked more scrambles than word searches.
2. They did as many mazes as crosswords and word searches combined.
3. They worked half as many scrambles as mazes.

|  | 8 | 12 | 16 | 20 | 24 |
|---|---|---|---|---|---|
| Crosswords |  |  |  |  |  |
| Mazes |  |  |  |  |  |
| Scrambles |  |  |  |  |  |
| Sudokus |  |  |  |  |  |
| Word Searches |  |  |  |  |  |

Use the grid to eliminate possibilities. Put an "x" in a box if a number doesn't go with a puzzle. Put an "o" if it does.

# 33. Countries Word Search

```
I  S  E  R  B  I  A  J
N  N  D  U  C  U  B  A
D  L  R  A  S  E  D  P
I  M  E  T  H  A  P  A
A  F  R  A  N  C  E  N
L  I  Z  A  R  B  R  A
A  J  C  P  A  S  U  H
L  I  T  I  A  H  I  G
```

Words go right, left, up, down, and diagonally.

| | | |
|---|---|---|
| AUSTRIA | CUBA | INDIA |
| BRAZIL | FIJI | ISRAEL |
| BURMA | FRANCE | JAPAN |
| CANADA | GHANA | PERU |
| CHAD | HAITI | SERBIA |

The uncircled letters spell another country: _____

# 34. Veggie Clues

Each word or phrase below is a clue for a small word found in the name of a vegetable. Can you list all the veggies? The first is done for you.

1. Pan **P O T** A T O

2. Taxi __ __ __ __ __ __ __

3. Decay __ __ __ __ __ __

4. Allow __ __ __ __ __ __ __

5. Either __ __ __ __

6. Atop __ __ __ __ __

7. Insect __ __ __ __

8. Plate __ __ __ __ __ __

9. Twirl __ __ __ __ __ __ __

10. Small rug __ __ __ __ __ __

11. Relative __ __ __ __ __ __ __

12. Tiny bite __ __ __ __ __ __

# 35. Kite Conundrum

The kites in each row, column, and the two main diagonals have something that's the same for them, but is different from the other six kites. Can you figure out what?

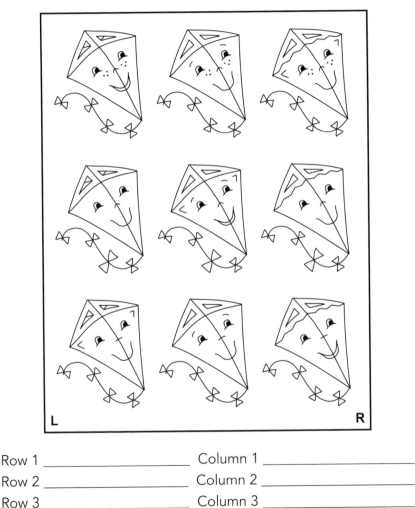

Row 1 _____   Column 1 _____
Row 2 _____   Column 2 _____
Row 3 _____   Column 3 _____
Diagonal L _____   Diagonal R _____

# 36. Hink Pinks

A *hink pink* is a pair of mystery 1-syllable rhyming words. A one-word clue is given for each part of the hink pink. An example is done for you. Can you do the rest?

1.  Distant sun _____**far star**_____

2.  Plump kitten _____

3.  Tidy road _____

4.  Crimson sleigh _____

5.  Rat abode _____

6.  Boat journey _____

7.  Ebony bag _____

8.  Unkind monarch _____

9.  Noisy group _____

10. Unusual seat _____

11. Metal tire _____

12. Twisted penny _____

13. Guaranteed healing _____

14. Garbage money _____

15. Pleasant herb _____

# 37. DOLPHIN Wordoku

Fill in the squares so that each row, column, and 7-square section has the letters D-O-L-P-H-I-N.

| I |   | O |   | N | L |   |
|---|---|---|---|---|---|---|
| L |   | P |   |   | D | O |
|   | O |   |   | H |   |   |
| P |   |   | O |   | H | D |
| O |   | D | I | P | N |   |
|   | P |   | N |   |   | L |
|   | D | H | L |   |   | I |

Adjusting difficulty level:
- To make the puzzle easier, have someone add letters from the answer key.
- To make it more challenging, have someone white out any or all of the letters shaded in the key.

# 38. Word Wrappers

For each blank use two or more of the letters in the underlined word to make a new word that will logically fit in the sentence. The letters in your new word must be in the same order as in the underlined word.

1. The recipe says to _____ _____ in the <u>sausage</u>.

2. The <u>ballad</u> was _____ about a _____ who attended a _____ and had a _____ experience.

3. I _____ <u>subjects</u> like _____ or _____ will be of interest to the kids.

4. _____ _____ <u>twenty</u> miles carrying our _____ and then hiked _____ more.

5. Just as the actor _____ a bell and _____ his opening lines, a <u>strange</u> _____ _____ onto the _____.

6. In our <u>lesson</u> _____ time, we learned an _____ is _____ than infinity.

7. I _____ the <u>chapter</u> in which the _____ wearing the red _____ and _____ saves the _____ and _____ in the runaway _____.

8. Whatever your _____, if all your arrows _____ in the <u>target</u> you _____ a _____ to eat.

# 39. Triangle Trails

Draw a path from the entry arrow to the exit arrow without going through any triangle more than once. A value in a cell tells the number of adjacent triangles (sharing a side) through which the path goes. The path cannot pass through a numbered cell.

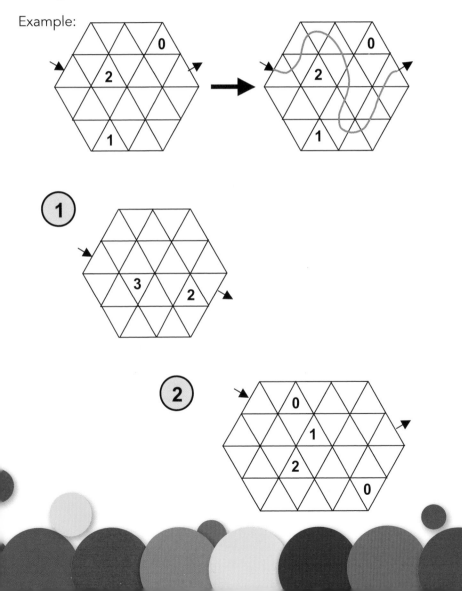

# 40. Coin Clue Puzzles

Using pennies, nickels, dimes, quarters, or half dollars, put the coins in the correct order according to the clues.

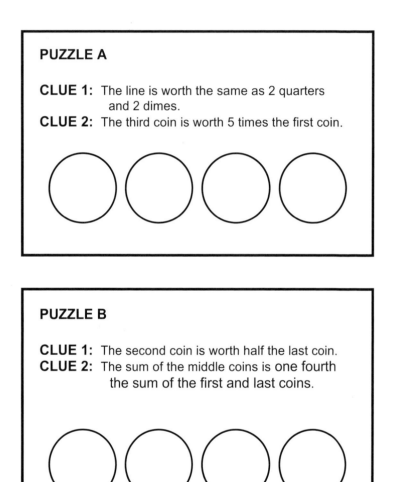

**PUZZLE A**

**CLUE 1:** The line is worth the same as 2 quarters and 2 dimes.
**CLUE 2:** The third coin is worth 5 times the first coin.

**PUZZLE B**

**CLUE 1:** The second coin is worth half the last coin.
**CLUE 2:** The sum of the middle coins is one fourth the sum of the first and last coins.

# 41. Ways to Travel Word Scramble

Spell another way to travel using the circled letters: _ _ _ _ _

# 42. Rhyme-It with SHARE

Many words rhyme with "SHARE." Below are clues for 30 of them. How many can you name and spell correctly?

1.  _ _ _ _ female horse

2.  _ _ _ _ _ set of steps

3.  _ _ _ _ rip

4.  _ _ _ _ rabbit

5.  _ _ _ _ _ seat

6.  _ _ _ _ challenge

7.  _ _ _ _ _ frighten

8.  _ _ _ _ fruit

9.  _ _ _ atmosphere

10. _ _ _ _ be concerned

11. _ _ _ _ two

12. _ _ _ _ scarce

13. _ _ _ _ _ trap

14. _ _ _ _ den

15. _ _ _ _ _ curse

16. _ _ _ _ _ loud noise

17. _ _ _ _ trim, shave off

18. _ _ _ _ have on

19. _ _ _ _ _ gaze fixedly

20. _ _ _ _ travel fee

21. _ _ _ _ _ _ _ announce

22. _ _ _ _ _ _ God talk

23. _ _ _ _ _ extra

24. _ _ _ _ _ gaze angrily

25. _ _ _ _ inheritor

26. _ _ _ _ _ blaze of light

27. _ _ _ _ _ _ fix

28. _ _ _ _ _ _ _ lose hope

29. _ _ _ _ _ conscious of

30. _ _ _ _ just, equitable

# 43. Word Search

| O | M | E | P | I | N | E | S |
|---|---|---|---|---|---|---|---|
| A | A | S | H | E | E | P | T |
| K | P | R | A | I | N | A | O |
| C | L | O | U | D | S | L | R |
| I | E | H | G | A | L | M | M |
| H | S | N | O | W | E | N | P |
| C | E | D | A | R | E | U | I |
| C | O | W | T | O | T | S | G |

Find words above that fit the categories given below.

| FARM ANIMALS | TREES | WEATHER |
|---|---|---|
| COW | | |
| | | |
| | | |
| | | |
| | | |
| | | |

# 44. Write-It-Right Puzzler

In each sentence the words that go in the two blanks are homophones. They are pronounced the same, but are spelled differently. Can you figure out the correct words?

1.  Mom made _ _ _ _ peach pies _ _ _ the party.

2.  He _ _ _ _ up the _ _ _ _ balloon the largest of all.

3.  She _ _ _ _ her bike down the _ _ _ _ to meet him.

4.  That was quite a _ _ _ _ to jump that many _ _ _ _ !

5.  The exhausted _ _ _ _ _ _ slept all _ _ _ _ _.

6.  I think _ _ _ play should last about an _ _ _ _.

7.  The _ _ _ _ of that kind of _ _ _ _ turns white in winter.

8.  Is this the _ _ _ that won _ _ _ a livestock ribbon?

9.  As flower girl, _ _ _ walk down the _ _ _ _ _ first.

10. We _ _ _  _ _ _ _ apple slices on the hike.

11. The teacher _ _ _ _ _ _ _ us to read our stories _ _ _ _ _.

12. Dad was too _ _ _ _ from the flu to work last _ _ _ _.

13. The _ _ _ _ _ of the skunk _ _ _ _ us scampering away as fast as possible.

14. _ _ _ _ _ you please find some _ _ _ _ for our campfire?

15. Ms. Lu wants _ _ _ to sing the _ _ _ _ as a solo.

*Need a hint? The answers are in this list:*
ate, night, aloud, wood, for, road, hour, you, blue, I'll, sent, him, feet, hair, week

# 45. Slippery Slopes

Fill in numbers, operation signs, or both, so that starting with the number in the top circle, then doing each operation as you come to it, brings you to the number in the last circle. Use only positive whole numbers.

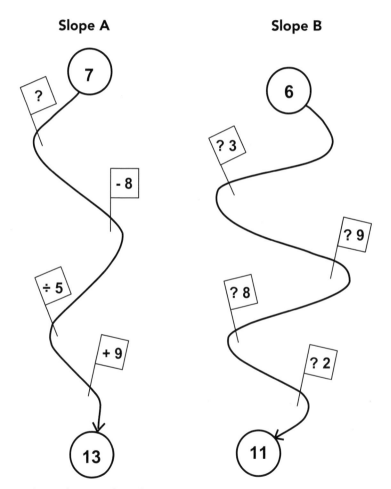

**Slope A**

**Slope B**

Find 2 solutions for Slope A.

# 46. Colored Dot Puzzles

Color the dots to match the clues.

**COLORED DOT**

**PUZZLE A**

**Clue 1:** A green dot is northeast of a red dot.

**Clue 2:** A blue dot is next to a red dot.

**Clue 3:** A red dot is northwest of a red dot.

**Clue 4:** A pink dot is southwest of a yellow dot.

**COLORED DOT**

**PUZZLE B**

**Clue 1:** A blue dot is due north of a green dot.

**Clue 2:** A red dot is between a green dot and a red dot.

**Clue 3:** A red dot is southwest of a green dot.

**Clue 4:** A blue dot is immediately west of a of a blue dot.

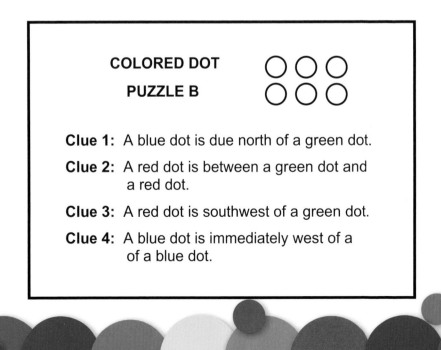

# 47. Careful Counting

How many triangles are in the figure at the right? _____

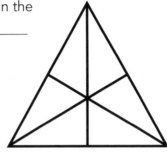

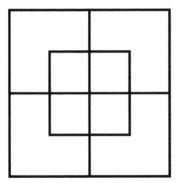

How many rectangles are in the figure at the left?

_____

(Don't forget that squares are a kind of rectangle.)

# 48. SKATING Wordoku

Fill in the squares so that each row, column, and 7-square section has the letters S-K-A-T-I-N-G.

|   | T | N |   | A |   |   |
|---|---|---|---|---|---|---|
|   | I |   | G | S | T |   |
| T |   | S | I |   |   | K |
| N | K |   |   | I | A |   |
|   |   | K | A |   |   | G |
|   | N |   |   | G | S |   |
| S |   | T |   |   | I | A |

Adjusting difficulty level:
- To make the puzzle easier, have someone add letters from the answer key.
- To make it more challenging, have someone white out any or all of the letters shaded in the key.

# 49. Know the Knitters?

Beth, Carter, Steve, and Tara knitted gifts for their friends. They each knitted a different item (cap, vest, blanket, and scarf) and each used a different color of yarn. Use the clues to decide who knitted each item and its color.

1. The cap is red.
2. Nobody made an item that started with the same letter as their name.
3. Steve did not choose a primary color.
4. The girl who made the green blanket finished her gift first.

|          | Beth | Carter | Steve | Tara | blue | brown | green | red |
|----------|------|--------|-------|------|------|-------|-------|-----|
| cap      |      |        |       |      |      |       |       |     |
| vest     |      |        |       |      |      |       |       |     |
| blanket  |      |        |       |      |      |       |       |     |
| scarf    |      |        |       |      |      |       |       |     |
| blue     |      |        |       |      |
| brown    |      |        |       |      |
| green    |      |        |       |      |
| red      |      |        |       |      |

Use the grid to eliminate possibilities. Put an "x" in a box if the two items do not go together. Put an "o" if they do.

# 50. How Sharp Are Your Eyes?

Find the two squares that have the symbols in exactly the same positions.

| | | | |
|---|---|---|---|
| ∇ Π<br>O Σ | O ∇<br>Π Σ | Π O<br>∇ Σ | ∇ Σ<br>O Π |
| Π Σ<br>∇ O | Σ Π<br>∇ O | O Π<br>∇ Σ | Π ∇<br>O Σ |
| Σ O<br>Π ∇ | Π ∇<br>Σ O | ∇ Π<br>Σ O | O Π<br>Σ ∇ |
| ∇ O<br>Π Σ | Σ Π<br>O ∇ | O ∇<br>Σ Π | Π Σ<br>O ∇ |
| Σ O<br>∇ Π | ∇ Σ<br>Π O | Π ∇<br>Σ O | ∇ O<br>Σ Π |

# 51. Triangle Trails

Draw a path from the entry arrow to the exit arrow without going through any triangle more than once. A value in a cell tells the number of adjacent triangles (sharing a side) through which the path goes. The path cannot pass through a numbered cell.

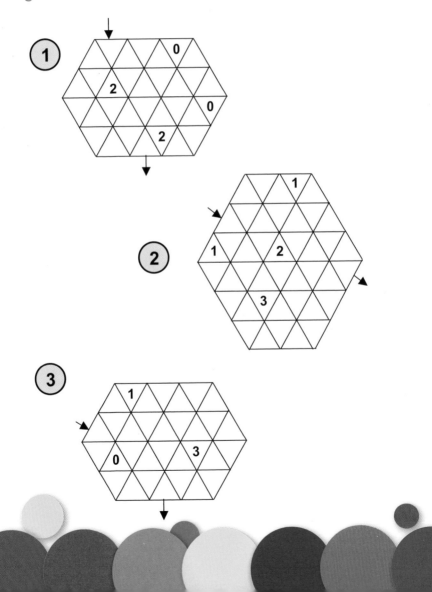

# 52. Target Equations: 16

Can you write 9 numerical expressions each of which equals **16**? Each expression may use only one kind of digit (1–9). You can't use more than 10 of the digit in the expression.

Challenge Level: use exactly 7 of the digit in each expression. (Example: number 4 has been done for you.)

| 1 | |
|---|---|
| 2 | |
| 3 | |
| 4 | **4 x (4 + 4/4) – 4 + 4 – 4 = 16** |
| 5 | |
| 6 | |
| 7 | |
| 8 | |
| 9 | |

# 53. Toothpick Teasers

Remove the specified number of toothpicks from the design so that the given number of squares are left. All remaining toothpicks must be part of a square. Squares may be different sizes.

A. Remove 4 toothpicks.
Leave 2 squares.

B. Remove 2 toothpicks.
Leave 2 squares.

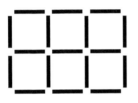

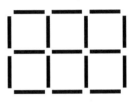

C. Remove 3 toothpicks.
Leave 4 small squares.

Remove 3 toothpicks.
Leave 4 small squares.

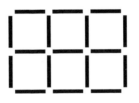

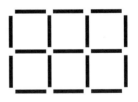

D. Remove 4 toothpicks.
Leave 3 squares.

Remove 4 toothpicks.
Leave 3 squares.

In C and D, find 2 *different* solutions. The solutions should not be just flips or rotations of each other.

# 54. Hidden Body Words

Find the name of a body part in each of the sentences below. The name will sometimes be part of more than one word.

1. We visited the farm to pick apples and choose a pumpkin.

2. Martin had to kneel down to enter the playhouse through the low door.

3. The monkeys scampered up the palm tree to get the coconuts.

4. A lawyer helped us with the legal decisions.

5. Jessica wrapped the ribbon around the box and then tied the bow.

6. Do you prefer a plum, a pear, or grapes for your snack?

7. The students had to pay a fee to attend the concert.

8. The graduate flung her cap into the air in joyous celebration.

9. I wanted to eat the whole carton of ice cream.

10. He addressed all the invitations to the party for us.

*Need a hint? The answers are in this list:*
*rib, knee, lung, head, arm, leg, toe, ear, palm, feet*

# 55. Word Search

```
C  R  I  C  K  E  T  E
I  E  P  I  N  K  F  G
T  B  P  F  U  N  L  N
N  L  U  I  H  A  Y  A
A  A  R  C  T  I  C  R
L  C  P  A  O  D  D  O
T  K  L  P  M  N  E  E
A (B  E  E) B  I  R  D
```

Find words above that fit the categories given below.

| INSECTS | OCEANS | COLORS |
|---------|--------|--------|
| BEE | | |
| | | |
| | | |
| | | |
| | | |

# 56. Word Builder for PELICAN

How many words, 3 letters or longer, can you spell using just the letters in the word "**PELICAN**"? Abbreviations, proper nouns, and foreign words are not allowed.

10—Good start!    25—Excellent!    40 or more—Outstanding!

# 57. Flower Word Scramble

Use the circled letters to spell another flower.

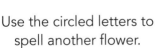

# 58. Rhyme-It with RAIL

Many words rhyme with "RAIL." Below are clues for 30 of them. How many can you name and spell correctly?

1. _ _ _ _ story

2. _ _ _ _ bucket

3. _ _ _ _ icy precipitation

4. _ _ _ _ travel by boat

5. _ _ _ _ be unsuccessful

6. _ _ _ _ prison

7. _ _ _ _ _ footpath

8. _ _ _ _ _ slug with a shell

9. _ _ _ _ _ weak

10. _ _ _ _ light colored

11. _ _ _ _ masculine

12. _ _ _ _ cry, howl

13. _ _ _ _ _ sea mammal

14. _ _ _ _ _ weighing device

15. _ _ _ _ small metal spike

16. _ _ _ _ _ _ old, tasteless

17. _ _ _ _ postal letters

18. _ _ _ _ bridal headwear

19. _ _ _ _ bargain prices

20. _ _ _ _ remove water

21. _ _ _ _ leafy vegetable

22. _ _ _ _ _ kind of bird

23. _ _ _ _ fit and hearty

24. _ _ _ _ rear appendage

25. _ _ _ be sick

26. _ _ _ _ strong wind

27. _ _ _ _ large bundle

28. _ _ _ _ _ flounder

29. _ _ _ _ _ _ individual fact

30. _ _ _ _ _ _ breathe out

# 59. Colored Dot Puzzles

Color the dots to match the clues.

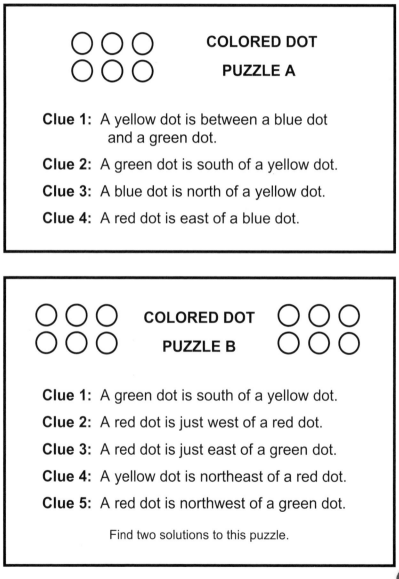

COLORED DOT

PUZZLE A

**Clue 1:** A yellow dot is between a blue dot and a green dot.

**Clue 2:** A green dot is south of a yellow dot.

**Clue 3:** A blue dot is north of a yellow dot.

**Clue 4:** A red dot is east of a blue dot.

COLORED DOT

PUZZLE B

**Clue 1:** A green dot is south of a yellow dot.

**Clue 2:** A red dot is just west of a red dot.

**Clue 3:** A red dot is just east of a green dot.

**Clue 4:** A yellow dot is northeast of a red dot.

**Clue 5:** A red dot is northwest of a green dot.

Find two solutions to this puzzle.

# 60. PUZZLES Wordoku

Fill in the squares so that each row, column, and 7-square section has the letters P-U-Z-Z-L-E-S (with 2 Zs in each).

| | | L | U | E | | Z |
|---|---|---|---|---|---|---|
| S | Z | | Z | | | L |
| E | L | | | P | Z | |
| | U | | Z | | E | |
| | Z | S | E | | | P |
| U | | P | | Z | Z | |
| Z | | U | | | L | Z |

Adjusting difficulty level:
- To make the puzzle easier, have someone add letters from the answer key.
- To make it more challenging, have someone white out any or all of the letters shaded in the key.

# 61. Slippery Slopes

Fill in numbers, operation signs, or both, so that starting with the number in the top circle, then doing each operation as you come to it, brings you to the number in the last circle. Use only positive whole numbers.

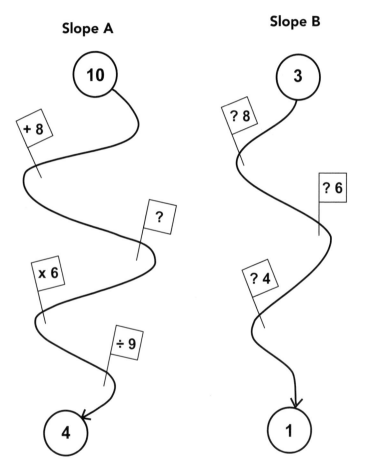

**Slope A**

10

+ 8

?

x 6

÷ 9

4

**Slope B**

3

? 8

? 6

? 4

1

Find 2 solutions for each slope.

# 62. Target Equations: 20

The target is **20**. Can you write 9 numerical expressions each of which equals 20? Each expression may use only one kind of digit (1–9). You can't use more than 10 of the digit in the expression.

Challenge Level: use exactly 7 of the digit in each expression. (Example: number 4 has been done for you.)

| | |
|---|---|
| **1** | |
| **2** | |
| **3** | |
| **4** | **(4 x 4) + 4 + (4/4) − (4/4) = 20** |
| **5** | |
| **6** | |
| **7** | |
| **8** | |
| **9** | |

# 63. Intersection Inquiry

Each shape has a different value. The numbers given in the puzzle are the value of that shape plus the values of any shapes that overlap it. Find the value of each shape and write it in the shape at the bottom. Don't guess. Have reasons for your answers.

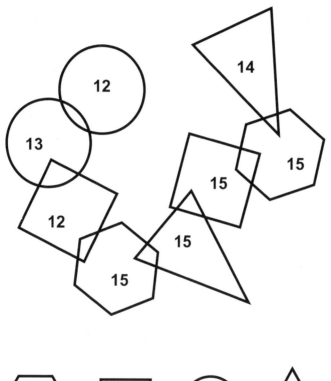

# 64. Hinky Pinkies

*Hinky pinkies* are similar to *hink pinks* (see page 38) except they are 2-syllable rhyming words. Below, the hinky pinkies have a (2) after the clues and the hink pinks have a (1).

1. Humorous rabbit (2)_____

2. Enjoyable gift (2)_____

3. Impolite quarrel (1)_____

4. Fake horse (2)_____

5. Cat glove (2)_____

6. Iron pot (2)_____

7. Hot hurricane (1)_____

8. Excellent sweets (2)_____

9. Foam difficulty (2)_____

10. Fantasy creek (1)_____

11. Tired question (2)_____

12. Fire smoke (1)_____

13. Gruesome tale (2)_____

14. Violin conundrum (2)_____

15. Dwarf book (1)_____

16. Hat poem (2)_____

# 65. Word Search

Find words that fit the categories given below.

| S | P | R | I | N | G | R | B |
|---|---|---|---|---|---|---|---|
| O | C | E | R | A | C | E | E |
| F | H | M | E | L | T | T | D |
| A | E | M | P | L | A | N | E |
| B | S | U | M | A | B | I | S |
| O | T | S | A | F | L | W | K |
| A | A | P | L | T | E | J | I |
| T | R | A | I | N | B | U | S |

**WAYS TO TRAVEL**

BUS

_____

_____

_____

_____

_____

**SEASONS**

_____

_____

_____

_____

**FURNITURE**

_____

_____

_____

_____

_____

# 66. CHAMPION Wordoku

Fill in the squares so that each row, column, and 8-square section has the letters C-H-A-M-P-I-O-N.

**1st**

| O |   | M | A |   | N |   | P |
|---|---|---|---|---|---|---|---|
| P | H |   |   | I |   |   | N |
|   | A | I |   | C |   | M | H |
| I |   | P | N |   | H | O |   |
|   |   | H | O | N |   | C | M |
| C | I |   |   | M | A |   | O |
|   | O | A | C |   |   | N |   |
| M |   |   | I |   | P | H |   |

Adjusting difficulty level:
- To make the puzzle easier, have someone add letters from the answer key.
- To make it more challenging, have someone white out any or all of the letters shaded in the key.

# 67. Toothpick Teasers

Remove the specified number of toothpicks from the design so that the given number of squares are left. All remaining toothpicks must be part of a square. Squares may be different sizes.

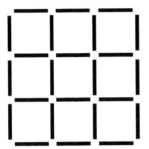

A.  Remove 4 toothpicks.
    Leave 5 squares.

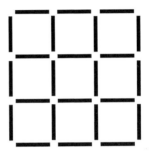

B.  Remove 8 toothpicks.
    Leave 5 squares.

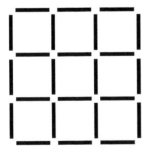

C.  Remove 8 toothpicks.
    Leave 2 squares.

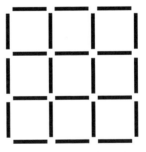

D.  Remove 8 toothpicks.
    Leave 3 squares.

    (Find two solutions.)

# 68. Hidden Body Words

Find the name of a body part in each of the sentences below. The name will usually be part of more than one word.

1. The clown's funny antics made us laugh and giggle.

2. It made no sense to buy another bike when Baker already had one.

3. My best friends live right down the street from me.

4. They exercise at the gym every day for an hour.

5. I love to visit the art museum when we go to New York.

6. She was definitely not in fashion wearing a drab raincoat and hat. (*This sentence has two.*)

7. Grandpa will visit his kin in Canada over the holidays.

8. The scout can rub one stick against another to start a fire.

9. I cannot hum both verses of the song without getting off key.

10. The music still sounds too loud from out here in the parking lot.

*Need a hint? The answers are in this list:*
ear, eye, hand, skin, heart, liver, thumb, bone, brain, mouth, nose

# 69. Country Word Scramble

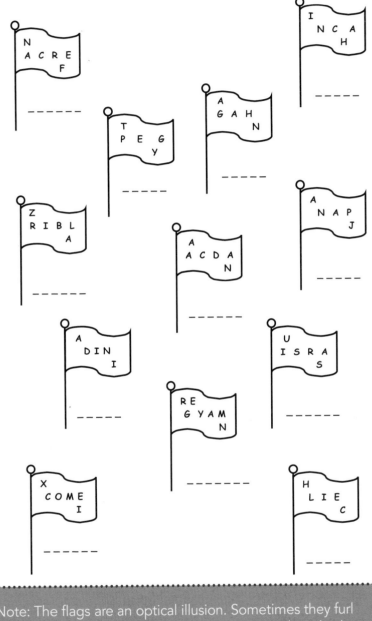

# 70. Word Builder for FLOWERS

How many words, 3 letters or longer, can you spell using just the letters in the word "**FLOWERS**"? Plurals are allowed but no abbreviations, proper nouns, or foreign words.

10—Good start!   20—Excellent!   30 or more—Outstanding!

# 71. Triangle Trails

Draw a path from the entry arrow to the exit arrow without going through any triangle more than once. A value in a cell tells the number of adjacent triangles (sharing a side) through which the path goes. The path cannot pass through a numbered cell.

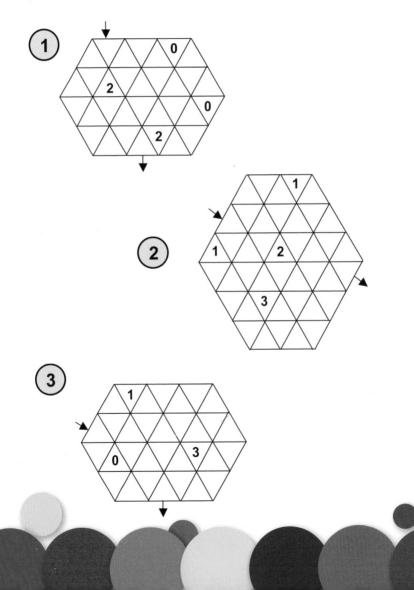

# 72. Rhyme-It with SPRAIN

Many words rhyme with "SPRAIN." Below are clues for 30 of them. How many can you name and spell correctly?

1. _ _ _ _ _ simple

2. _ _ _ _ horse hair

3. _ _ _ _ narrow road

4. _ _ _ _ get

5. _ _ _ _ walking stick

6. _ _ _ _ hurt, ache

7. _ _ _ _ _ thinking organ

8. _ _ _ _ _ metal links

9. _ _ _ _ _ jet

10. _ _ _ _ blood vessel

11. _ _ _ _ major

12. _ _ _ _ _ window glass

13. _ _ _ _ _ killed

14. _ _ _ _ _ locomotive

15. _ _ _ _ precipitation

16. _ _ _ _ _ discolor, spot

17. _ _ _ _ _ _ mentally ill

18. _ _ _ _ _ empty liquid

19. _ _ _ _ _ derrick

20. _ _ _ _ _ rule

21. _ _ _ _ _ cereal crop

22. _ _ _ _ _ _ overwork

23. _ _ _ _ conceited

24. _ _ _ _ bridle part

25. _ _ _ _ _ _ _ hold

26. _ _ _ _ _ _ _ make clear

27. _ _ _ _ _ _ stay, endure

28. _ _ _ _ _ _ _ _ gripe

29. _ _ _ _ decline, diminish

30. _ _ _ _ _ _ empire

# 73. Intersection Inquiry

Each shape has a different value. The numbers given in the puzzle are the value of that shape plus the values of any shapes that overlap it. Find the value of each shape and write it in the shape at the bottom. Don't guess. Have reasons for your answers.

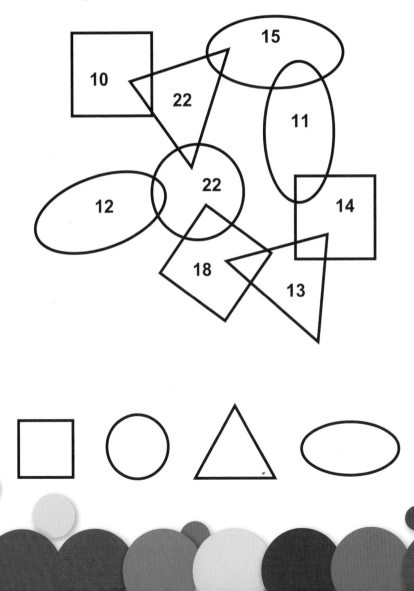

# 74. Target Equations: 25

The target is **25**. Can you write 9 numerical expressions each of which equals 25? Each expression may use only one kind of digit (1–9). You can't use more than 10 of the digit in the expression.

Challenge Level: use exactly 7 of the digit in each expression. (Example: number 4 has been done for you.)

| 1 | |
|---|---|
| 2 | |
| 3 | |
| 4 | $4 \times (4+4) - 4 - 4 + 4/4 = 25$ |
| 5 | |
| 6 | |
| 7 | |
| 8 | |
| 9 | |

# 75. Venn Puzzler

The fairy tale princess is having a ball to honor the magical wee ones who are her friends. She only invites guests who have seen elves or pixies or brownies or more than one kind of these creatures.

- She invites 180 guests.
- 60 have seen brownies.
- 100 have seen elves.
- 55 have seen only elves.
- 5 have seen all three.
- 25 have seen only brownies.
- 35 have seen pixies and elves.

How many invited guests have seen pixies? _____
How many have seen only pixies? _____

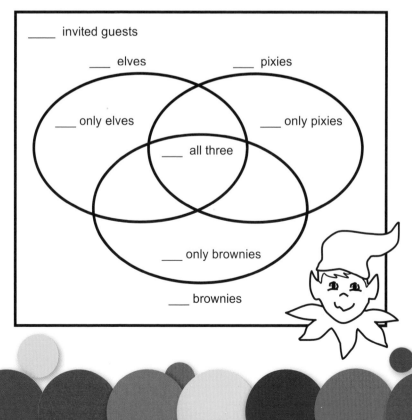

____ invited guests

____ elves          ____ pixies

____ only elves          ____ only pixies

____ all three

____ only brownies

____ brownies

# 76. DRAGONS Wordoku

Fill in the squares so that each row, column, and 7-square section has the letters D-R-A-G-O-N-S.

| O | G |   |   | A |   | N |
|---|---|---|---|---|---|---|
|   |   | R | S | D |   | G |
| S | D | G |   | N |   |   |
| A |   |   | N |   | G |   |
|   | O |   | D |   | A | R |
|   | R | A |   | O |   |   |
| R |   |   | O |   | D | A |

Adjusting difficulty level:
* To make the puzzle easier, have someone add letters from the answer key.
* To make it more challenging, have someone white out any or all of the letters shaded in the key.

# 77. Slippery Slopes

Fill in the operation signs, so that starting with the number in the top circle, then doing each operation as you come to it, brings you to the number in the last circle. Use only positive whole numbers.

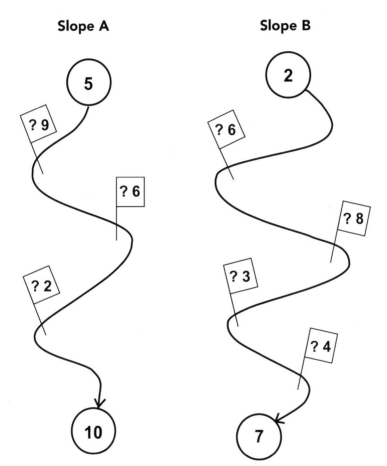

**Slope A**

5

? 9

? 6

? 2

10

**Slope B**

2

? 6

? 8

? 3

? 4

7

Find 2 solutions for each slope.

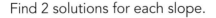

# 78. Word Search

Find words that fit the categories given below.

| | | | | | | |
|---|---|---|---|---|---|---|
| J | U | P | I | T | E | R | Y |
| T | S | L | S | O | N | E | R |
| E | U | I | U | H | U | M | U |
| N | N | E | N | C | T | M | C |
| I | E | R | A | N | P | A | R |
| N | V | S | R | E | E | H | E |
| S | A | T | U | R | N | O | M |
| X | I | S | A | W | O | W | T |

**PLANETS**      **TOOLS**      **NUMBERS**

_____      _____      ____SIX____

_____      _____      _____

_____      _____      _____

_____      _____      _____

_____      _____

_____

# 79. Travel Teaser

Anne, Ross, Maria, and Scott traveled to four different states and did different activities: they went to a zoo, a museum, an amusement park, and a campground. Use the clues to decide which state each visited and what they did.

1. Ross traveled east of the person at the amusement park.
2. A girl camped in the Rocky Mountains.
3. The zoo that was visited was in the largest of the four states.
4. Maria and a boy shared pictures they took west of the Mississippi River.

|  | Anne | Ross | Maria | Scott | CA | GA | CO | IL |
|---|---|---|---|---|---|---|---|---|
| park |  |  |  |  |  |  |  |  |
| campground |  |  |  |  |  |  |  |  |
| museum |  |  |  |  |  |  |  |  |
| zoo |  |  |  |  |  |  |  |  |
| CA |  |  |  |  |  |  |  |  |
| GA |  |  |  |  |  |  |  |  |
| CO |  |  |  |  |  |  |  |  |
| IL |  |  |  |  |  |  |  |  |

Use the grid to eliminate possibilities. Put an "x" in a box if the two items do not go together. Put an "o" if they do.

# 80. Intersection Inquiry

Each shape has a different value. The numbers given in the puzzle are the value of that shape plus the values of any shapes that overlap it. Find the value of each shape and write it in the shape at the bottom. Don't guess. Have reasons for your answers.

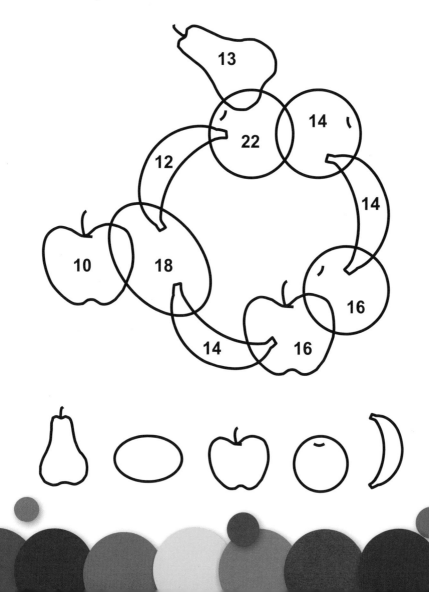

# 81. Toothpick Teasers

Move the specified number of toothpicks to a different part of the design so the given number of squares are left. All toothpicks must be part of a square.

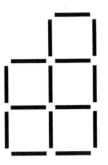

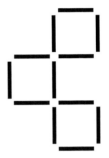

A. Move 3 toothpicks.
   Leave 4 squares.

B. Move 3 toothpicks.
   Leave 5 squares.

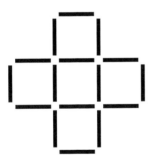

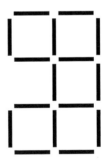

C. Move 4 toothpicks.
   Leave 4 squares.

D. Move 2 toothpicks.
   Leave 8 squares.

Note: D is tricky. Consider it an extra challenge!

# 82. Hidden Fruits

Find the name of a fruit in each of the sentences below. The name will usually be part of more than one word. Ignore capitals.

1. Where did the man go who helped us rescue our kitten?

2. If you work around loud machinery, stop ear damage by wearing earplugs.

3. The instructions say not to staple money to the order form.

4. On her vacation, she wants to go live in a tree house.

5. Each week I wish upon a different star and hope my dreams come true.

6. Can you figure out the puzzle without the extra clues?

7. Rachel told me long before it was in the newspaper that she had won the contest.

8. When I do my magic trick, cheer and clap, please.

9. Clara will snap each lid on a jar of honey after she has written the date on it. (*This has two fruits in it.*)

10. Lane slipped the check into a slim envelope to give to the plumber. (*This has two fruits in it.*)

*Need a hint? The answers are in this list:*
apple, date, pear, peach, lemon, lime, mango, plum, olive, melon, kiwi, fig

# 83. Careful Counting

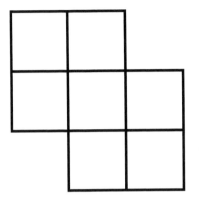

How many rectangles are
in the figure at the left?

_____

(Don't forget that squares are
a kind of rectangle.)

How many triangles are
in the figure at the right?

_____

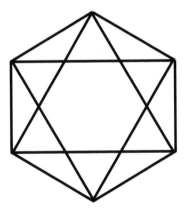

# 84. Water for the Wizard

The wizard is concocting some new potions. He sends you to the stream to get him some magical water, but he only gives you a 7-cup container and a 3-cup container.

A. The first time he asks for *exactly* 1 cup of water. How do you do it?

B. The next time he asks for *exactly* 2 cups of water. How do you do it?

C. The last time he asks for *exactly* 5 cups of water. How do you do it?

(No estimating allowed.)

# 85. COGITATE Wordoku

Cogitate means to think deeply. Fill in the squares so that each row, column, and 8-square section has the letters C-O-G-I-T-A-T-E (two T's in each).

| A |   |   | G |   | T |   | I |
|---|---|---|---|---|---|---|---|
|   | T | C | T |   |   | E |   |
|   |   | A |   | I | G | T |   |
|   | C | T | O |   | E | G |   |
| T |   | T |   | C |   | A |   |
|   | O |   | I | T |   | T | E |
| T | G |   |   | O | T |   |   |
| E |   | I | T |   | C |   | T |

Adjusting difficulty level:
- To make the puzzle easier, have someone add some letters from the answer key.
- To make it more challenging, have someone white out any or all of the letters shaded in the key.

# 86. Word Search

Find words that fit the categories given below.

| R | E | K | R | A | M | D | M |
|---|---|---|---|---|---|---|---|
| E | G | N | A | R | O | A | E |
| T | R | T | N | O | M | E | L |
| U | A | S | K | I | N | H | O |
| P | P | E | L | P | P | A | N |
| M | E | H | E | T | O | O | F |
| O | A | C | Q | U | I | L | L |
| C | R | A | Y | O | N | E | P |

**WRITING TOOLS**     **FRUITS**     **BODY PARTS**

_____   _____   _____

_____   _____   _____

_____   _____   _____

_____   _____   _____

_____   _____   _____

                    _____

# 87. Triangle Trails

Draw a path from the entry arrow to the exit arrow without going through any triangle more than once. A value in a cell tells the number of adjacent triangles (sharing a side) through which the path goes. The path cannot pass through a numbered cell.

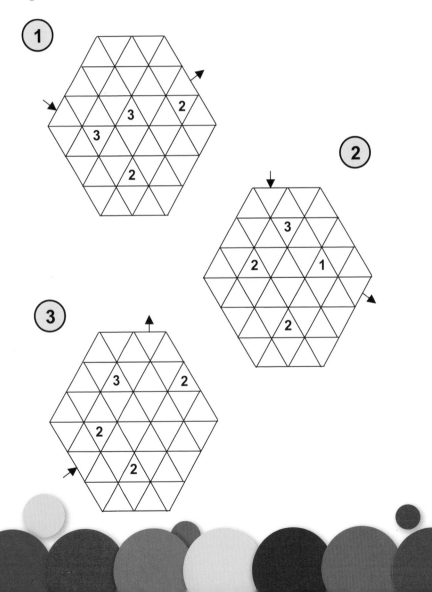

# 88. Slippery Slopes

Fill in the operation signs, so that starting with the number in the top circle, then doing each operation as you come to it, brings you to the number in the last circle. Use only positive whole numbers.

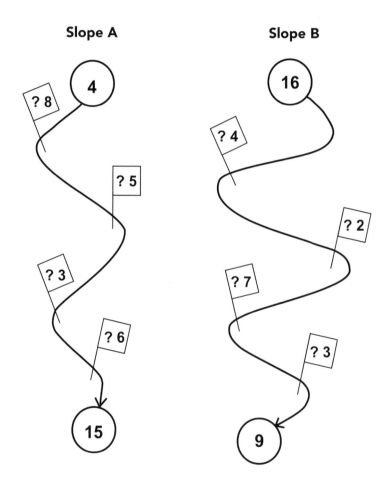

**Slope A**

**Slope B**

Find 2 solutions for each slope.

# 89. Intersection Inquiry

Each shape has a different value. The numbers given in the puzzle are the value of that shape plus the values of any shapes that overlap it. Find the value of each shape and write it in the shape at the bottom. Don't guess. Have reasons for your answers.

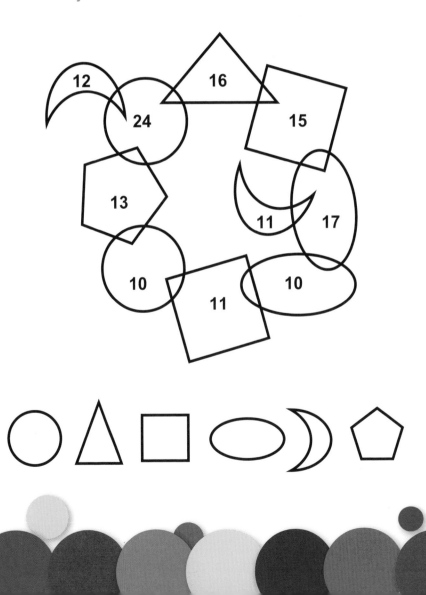

# 90. Target Equations: 30

The target is **30**. Can you write 9 numerical expressions each of which equals 30? Each expression may use only one kind of digit (1–9). You can't use more than 10 of the digit in the expression.

Challenge Level: use exactly 7 of the digit in each expression. (Example: number 4 has been done for you.)

| 1 | |
|---|---|
| 2 | |
| 3 | |
| 4 | $4 + (4 \times 4) + (44 - 4)/4 = 30$ |
| 5 | |
| 6 | |
| 7 | |
| 8 | |
| 9 | |

# 91. Present Puzzler

Draw a line from each person to their present. Your lines may not cross each other, go through a gift, or go outside the large box.

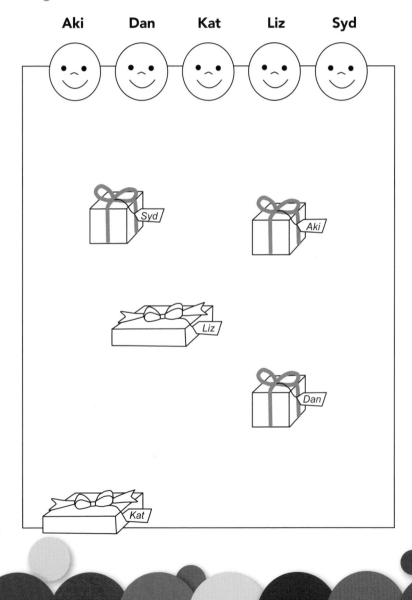

# 92. LAUGHTER Wordoku

Fill in the squares so that each row, column, and 8-square section has the letters L-A-U-G-H-T-E-R.

| | | L | R | E | A | | |
|---|---|---|---|---|---|---|---|
| A | | H | U | G | | | T |
| U | | R | T | | E | H | |
| | A | | | H | | E | R |
| G | T | | | R | | A | L |
| H | R | | E | | G | | U |
| | H | G | | U | R | T | |
| R | | T | A | | | G | E |

Adjusting difficulty level:
- To make the puzzle easier, have someone add letters from the answer key.
- To make it more challenging, have someone white out any or all of the letters shaded in the key.

# 93. Venn Puzzler

This week the sixth graders fixed lunches for the homeless in their community. They made ham sandwiches with optional additions of: mustard, cheese, and lettuce. Use the facts given below to find out how many sandwiches they made.

- 16 sandwiches had cheese.
- 11 sandwiches had mustard.
- 3 sandwiches had only lettuce.
- 5 sandwiches had mustard, cheese, and lettuce.
- 2 sandwiches had mustard and lettuce but not cheese.
- 3 sandwiches had mustard and cheese but not lettuce.
- 1 more sandwich had only cheese than had only lettuce.
- Twice as many sandwiches had nothing extra as had only mustard.

How many sandwiches did the group make? _____

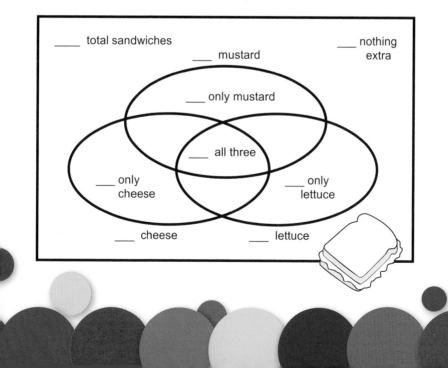

# 94. Country Conundrums

Find the name of a country in each of the sentences below. The name will often be part of more than one word.

1.  The old man has pains in his back and shoulders.

2.  Can a daisy grow in sandy soil?

3.  Recycled paper uses fewer trees.

4.  We had turkey and dressing for Thanksgiving.

5.  The immigrants think their new country is a nice land.

6.  The teacher gave us the information in diagrams and graphs.

7.  Each of us has one pal to keep us company on the trip.

8.  The gazelle ran through a narrow opening in the wall.

9.  The mother bear gave her cub a piece of fruit.

10. The baby looked funny with cereal on her chin and banana in her hair.

*Need a hint? The hidden countries are in this list:*
*India, China, Peru, Cuba, Iceland, Turkey, Canada, Nepal, Ghana, Spain*

# 95. Slippery Slopes

Fill in the operation signs, so that starting with the number in the top circle, then doing each operation as you come to it, brings you to the number in the last circle. Use only positive whole numbers.

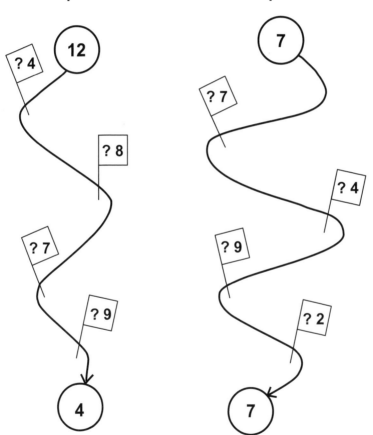

Find 5 solutions for Slope B.

# 96. Rhyme-It with PLIGHT

Many words rhyme with "PLIGHT." Below are clues for 30 of them. How many can you name and spell correctly?

1. _ _ _ _ _ not day

2. _ _ _ _ _ correct

3. _ _ _ _ _ use a pen

4. _ _ _ _ flying toy

5. _ _ _ _ _ vision

6. _ _ _ _ _ _ fear

7. _ _ _ _ use your teeth

8. _ _ _ _ _ colorless

9. _ _ _ _ _ not loose

10. _ _ _ _ _ wage war

11. _ _ _ _ _ strength, power

12. _ _ _ _ _ _ tallness

13. _ _ _ _ _ _ elf, pixie

14. _ _ _ _ _ _ chess piece

15. _ _ _ _ _ illumination

16. _ _ _ _ _ _ brilliant

17. _ _ _ _ _ _ air travel

18. _ _ _ _ _ _ tiny, modest

19. _ _ _ _ _ join together

20. _ _ _ _ _ _ courteous

21. _ _ _ _ _ _ set fire to

22. _ _ _ _ _ desire to hurt

23. _ _ _ _ ceremony

24. _ _ _ _ location, place

25. _ _ _ _ 8-legged critter

26. _ _ _ _ _ _ _ thrill, charm

27. _ _ _ _ _ _ repeat aloud

28. _ _ _ _ _ _ _ _ explosive

29. _ _ _ _ _ completely

30. _ _ _ _ _ overused

# 97. Triangle Trails

Draw a path from the entry arrow to the exit arrow without going through any triangle more than once. A value in a cell tells the number of adjacent triangles (sharing a side) through which the path goes. The path cannot pass through a numbered cell.

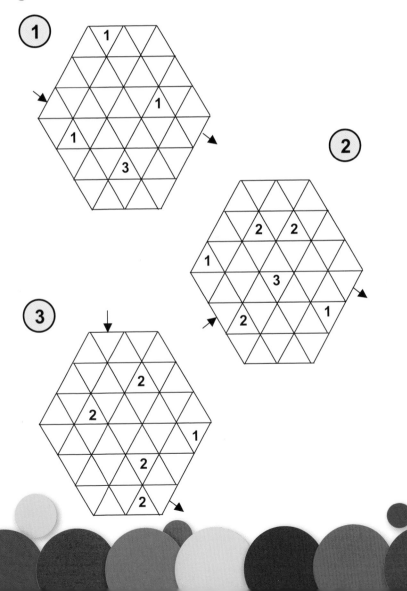

# 98. Target Equations: 36

The target is **36.** Can you write 9 numerical expressions each of which equals 36? Each expression may use only one kind of digit (1–9). You can't use more than 10 of the digit in the expression.

Challenge Level: use exactly 7 of the digit in each expression. (Example: number 8 has been done for you.)

| | |
|---|---|
| **1** | |
| **2** | |
| **3** | |
| **4** | |
| **5** | |
| **6** | |
| **7** | |
| **8** | 8/(8+8) x 8 x (8 + 8/8) = 36 |
| **9** | |

# 99. Intersection Inquiry

Each shape has a different value. The numbers given in the puzzle are the value of that shape plus the values of any shapes that overlap it. Find the value of each shape and write it in the shape at the bottom. Don't guess. Have reasons for your answers.

# 100. Category Challenge

For this puzzle, think of a word for each category on the left which starts with the letter at the top. Don't repeat any words. You're allowed four blank boxes.

|  | M | E | N | S | A |
|---|---|---|---|---|---|
| 4-letter words |  |  |  |  |  |
| Vegetables or fruits |  |  |  |  |  |
| Verbs |  |  |  |  |  |
| Bodies of water |  |  |  |  |  |
| Birds |  |  |  |  |  |
| Animals (not birds) |  |  |  |  |  |
| Body parts |  |  |  |  |  |
| Flowers or trees |  |  |  |  |  |
| Countries |  |  |  |  |  |
| Things in the solar system |  |  |  |  |  |

# Answers

[Note: Some puzzles may have additional solutions to those given here.]

**1.**

| + | 3 | 7 |
|---|---|---|
| 5 | 8 | 12 |
| 2 | 5 | 9 |
| 6 | 9 | 13 |

| + | 2 | 8 | 4 |
|---|---|---|---|
| 4 | 6 | 12 | 8 |
| 3 | 5 | 11 | 7 |
| 9 | 11 | 17 | 13 |

**2.**

| 2 | 4 | 7 | 13 |
|---|---|---|---|
| 3 | 0 | 6 | 9 |
| 1 | 8 | 5 | 14 |
| 6 | 12 | 18 | 36 |

| 9 | 1 | 3 | 13 |
|---|---|---|---|
| 3 | 4 | 1 | 8 |
| 0 | 6 | 5 | 11 |
| 12 | 11 | 9 | 32 |

**3.**
Cal—cooking pot; Ling—cowboy hat; Mirka—baseball cap; Will—top hat

**4.**
1. be, bars
2. pope, pole
3. How, he, me
4. ever, lever
5. sigh, sit, it
6. or, for, fort
7. lad, lead
8. late, sat, ate

**5.**
Alexandra—5; Carly—1; Eliza—3; Georgina—2; Tyler—4

**6.**

| + | 17 | 9 |
|---|---|---|
| 12 | 29 | 21 |
| 14 | 31 | 23 |
| 8 | 25 | 17 |

| + | 15 | 7 | 16 |
|---|---|---|---|
| 18 | 33 | 25 | 34 |
| 9 | 24 | 16 | 25 |
| 13 | 28 | 20 | 29 |

**7.**
5, 6, 5

**8.**

| 7 | 4 | 4 | 15 |
|---|---|---|---|
| 2 | 3 | 6 | 11 |
| 5 | 6 | 1 | 12 |
| 14 | 13 | 11 | 38 |

| 1 | 6 | 2 | 9 |
|---|---|---|---|
| 3 | 8 | 4 | 15 |
| 9 | 0 | 7 | 16 |
| 13 | 14 | 13 | 40 |

**9.**
MARS, PLUTO, VENUS, COMET, URANUS, EARTH, JUPITER, NEPTUNE, METEOR, PLANET, MERCURY, SATURN

**10.** (Possible answers—not a complete list)
ace(s), act(s), ale(s), ate, case, cast(e), cat(s), cleat(s), east, eat(s), lace(s), lase, last, late, lea(s)(t), lest, let(s), sac, sale, salt, sat(e), scale, scat, seal, sea(t), sect, set(a), slat(e), stale, steal, talc(s), tale(s), tea(s), teal(s)

**11.**

| 4 | 5 | 6 | 7 | 8 | 9 |
|---|---|---|---|---|---|
| 8 | 7 | 9 | 6 | 4 | 5 |
| 5 | 9 | 4 | 8 | 6 | 7 |
| 6 | 8 | 7 | 9 | 5 | 4 |
| 9 | 6 | 5 | 4 | 7 | 8 |
| 7 | 4 | 8 | 5 | 9 | 6 |

**12.**

| X | 2 | 6 |
|---|---|---|
| 6 | 12 | 36 |
| 3 | 6 | 18 |
| 4 | 8 | 24 |

| X | 9 | 3 | 6 |
|---|---|---|---|
| 8 | 72 | 24 | 48 |
| 4 | 36 | 12 | 24 |
| 2 | 18 | 6 | 12 |

**13.**

| N | S | M | A | E |
|---|---|---|---|---|
| A | M | E | N | S |
| E | A | S | M | N |
| M | E | N | S | A |
| S | N | A | E | M |

**14.**
Meg—oak; John—pear; Sarah—apple; Zeke—maple

**15.**
**A.** B R G B          **B.** Y G B R

**16.**

| X | 8 | 4 |
|---|---|---|
| 5 | 40 | 20 |
| 8 | 64 | 32 |
| 7 | 56 | 28 |

| X | 7 | 3 | 9 |
|---|---|---|---|
| 6 | 42 | 18 | 54 |
| 9 | 63 | 27 | 81 |
| 5 | 35 | 15 | 45 |

**17.**

Row 1: ears

Row 2: socks

Row 3: hairs

Column 1: buckles

Column 2: fingers

Column 3: teeth

Diagonal L: eye

Diagonal R: toes

**18.**
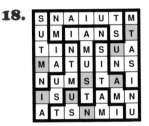

**19.**

1. us, use, hoe
2. hem, her, it
3. We, owe, lower, for
4. get, in, tin

5. pay, part, art, at
6. We, omen, won, men
7. pie, is, sure
8. man, mare, mane

**20.**

Anna—8; Chloe—4; Felix—10; Juan—5; Miguel—7

**21.**

CRICKET, FLIES, MOTH, BEETLE, FLEA, ROACH, WASP, LADYBUG, LICE, LOCUST, APHID, TERMITE, CICADA

**22.**

**A.** - 6

**B.** ( ÷ + - )

**23.**
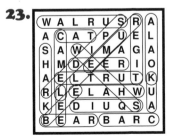

**24.**

The last square in Row 1 and the first square in Row 3

**25.**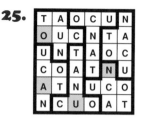

**26.**

**A.** N Q N D

**B.** P N D D

**27.** (Possible answers—not a complete list)
ale(s), ant(s), ante, ate, east, eat(s), lane(s), last, late(st), latent, latte(s), lea(s)(t), lean(s), lens, lent, lest, let(s), neat, nest, net(s), sale, salt, sane, sat(e), sea(l), seat, sent, set, seta, slant, slat(e), stale, state, steal, stent, tale(nt), tales, tan(s), taste, tea(l)(s), teat(s), ten(s), tent(s), test

**28.**

1. tale, able
2. peal, pal(s), pet(s)
3. No, ice, not
4. camper, came, car, camp

5. date, cat, eat
6. hard, hear, ear, he, had
7. run, urn
8. pants, hat, let, lean, pat

**29.**
3, 18

**30.**

| | | | |
|---|---|---|---|
| 1. dry | 9. fly | 17. shy | 25. reply |
| 2. pie | 10. lie | 18. tie | 26. thigh |
| 3. cry | 11. dye | 19. why | 27. try |
| 4. high | 12. sky | 20. pry | 28. ally |
| 5. buy | 13. rye | 21. sly | 29. rely |
| 6. sty | 14. fry | 22. bye | 30. lullaby |
| 7. die | 15. spy | 23. deny | |
| 8. eye | 16. guy | 24. spry | |

**31.**

C (the moon covers part of the big oval)

## 32.

Crosswords—16; Mazes—24; Scrambles—12; Sudokus—20; Word searches—8

## 33.

NEPAL

## 34.

| | | |
|---|---|---|
| 1. POTATO | 5. CORN | 9. SPINACH |
| 2. CABBAGE | 6. ONION | 10. TOMATO |
| 3. CARROT | 7. BEET | 11. PUMPKIN |
| 4. LETTUCE | 8. RADISH | 12. TURNIP |

## 35.

Row 1: freckles          Column 1: triangles    Diagonal L: ears
Row 2: bigger bow        Column 2: eyebrows     Diagonal R: smile
Row 3: nose              Column 3: crossbar

## 36.

| | | |
|---|---|---|
| 1. far star | 6. ship trip | 11. steel wheel |
| 2. fat cat | 7. black sack | 12. bent cent |
| 3. neat street | 8. mean queen | 13. sure cure |
| 4. red sled | 9. loud crowd | 14. trash cash |
| 5. mouse house | 10. rare chair | 15. nice spice |

## 37.

## 38.

1. use, sage
2. all, lad, ball, bad
3. bet, jets, subs
4. We, went, tent, ten
5. rang, sang, stag, ran, stage

6. on, eon, less
7. hate, chap, cape, hat, ape, cat, car
8. age, are, get, tart

## 39.

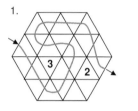
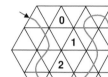

## 40.

**A.** D N H N

**B.** H N D D

## 41.

PLANE, HORSE, TRAIN, SKATES, CANOE, BALLOON, BICYCLE, SUBWAY, ROWBOAT, WAGON, ROCKET, CAMEL, TRUCK

## 42.

1. mare
2. stair
3. tear
4. hare
5. chair
6. dare
7. scare
8. pear
9. air
10. care
11. pair
12. rare
13. snare
14. lair
15. swear
16. blare
17. pare
18. wear
19. stare
20. fare
21. declare
22. prayer
23. spare
24. glare
25. heir
26. flare
27. repair
28. despair
29. aware
30. fair

## 43.

**FARM ANIMALS:** SHEEP, CHICK, [COW], PIG, GOAT, HORSE
**TREES:** OAK, MAPLE, PINE, CEDAR, PALM
**WEATHER:** RAIN, CLOUDS, SNOW, SUN, STORM, SLEET

## 44.

1. four, for
2. blew, blue
3. rode, road
4. feat, feet
5. knight, night
6. our, hour
7. hair, hare
8. ewe, you
9. I'll, aisle
10. ate, eight
11. allowed, aloud
12. weak, week
13. scent, sent
14. Would, wood
15. him, hymn

## 45.

**A.** x 4, + 21

**B.** ( + ÷ + + )

## 46.

**A.** R Y G
   P R B

**B.** B B G
   G R R

## 47.

16, 18

## 48.

| G | T | N | S | A | K | I |
|---|---|---|---|---|---|---|
| K | I | A | G | S | T | N |
| T | A | S | I | N | G | K |
| N | K | G | T | I | A | S |
| I | S | K | A | T | N | G |
| A | N | I | K | G | S | T |
| S | G | T | N | K | I | A |

## 49.

Beth: red cap; Carter: blue scarf; Steve: brown vest; Tara: green blanket

## 50.

The second square in Row 3 and the third square in Row 5

## 51.

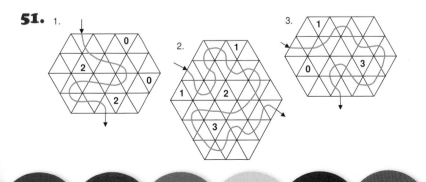

## 52.

Sample solutions:

1. 11 + 1+1+1+1+1

2. 22/2 + 2 + 2 + 2/2

3. 3 + 3 + 3 + 3 + 3 + 3/3

4. 4 x (4 + 4/4) - 4 + 4 - 4

5. 5 + 5 + 5 + 5/5 + 5 - 5

6. 6 + 6 + 6 - 6/6 - 6/6

7. 7+7+7 - 7 + (7+7)/7

8. (8 + 8) x [(8+8)/8- 8/8]

9. 9 + 9 - (9+9)/9 + 9 - 9

## 53.

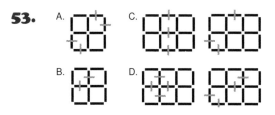

## 54.

1. arm
2. knee
3. palm
4. leg
5. rib
6. ear
7. feet
8. lung
9. toe
10. head

## 55.

**INSECTS:** [BEE], ANT, CRICKET, MOTH, FLY
**OCEANS:** ATLANTIC, PACIFIC, INDIAN, ARCTIC
**COLORS:** BLACK, PINK, RED, ORANGE, PURPLE

**56.** (Possible answers—not a complete list)
ace, acne, ail, ale, alien, alp(ine), can(e), cap(e), clan, clap, clean, clip, elan, epic, lace, lain, lance, lane, lap(el), lea(n), leap, lie(n), lice, line, lip, nail, nap(e), neap, nice, nip, pail, pain, pal(e), pan(e), panel, panic, peal, pecan, pen(cil), pica, pie, pile, pine, place, plan(e), plea

## 57.

ROSE, IRIS, DAISY, TULIP, CROCUS, BEGONIA, LILAC, ORCHID, PANSY, PETUNIA, PEONY, ASTER, POPPY

## 58.

| | | | |
|---|---|---|---|
| 1. tale | 9. frail | 17. mail | 25. ail |
| 2. pail | 10. pale | 18. veil | 26. gale |
| 3. hail | 11. male | 19. sale | 27. bale |
| 4. sail | 12. wail | 20. bail | 28. flail |
| 5. fail | 13. whale | 21. kale | 29. detail |
| 6. jail | 14. scale | 22. quail | 30. exhale |
| 7. trail | 15. nail | 23. hale | |
| 8. snail | 16. stale | 24. tail | |

## 59.

**A.** Y B R
　  G Y B

**B.** R R Y
　  G R G

G R Y
R R G

## 60.

| Z | P | L | U | E | S | Z |
|---|---|---|---|---|---|---|
| S | Z | E | Z | U | P | L |
| E | L | Z | S | P | Z | U |
| P | U | Z | Z | L | E | S |
| L | Z | S | E | Z | U | P |
| U | S | P | L | Z | Z | E |
| Z | E | U | P | S | L | Z |

## 61.

**A.** ÷ 3, - 12

**B.** ( + - - ) ( x ÷ ÷ )

## 62.

Sample solutions:

1. (1 x 11) + 11 − 1 − 1

2. (2/2) x 22 − [(2/2) x 2]

3. 3 x (3 + 3) + 3/3 + 3/3

4. (4 x 4) + 4 + (4/4) - (4/4)

5. (5 x 5) − 5 + 5/5 − 5/5

6. 6 + 6 + 6 + 6/6 + 6/6

7. 7+7+7 − (7/7 x 7/7)

8. 8 + 8 + (8+8+8+8)/8

9. 9 + 9 + (9+9)/9 + 9 − 9

## 63.

5, 1, 6, 9

## 64.

1. funny bunny
2. pleasant present
3. rude feud
4. phony pony
5. kitten mitten
6. metal kettle
7. warm storm
8. dandy candy
9. bubble trouble
10. dream stream
11. weary query
12. blaze haze
13. gory story
14. fiddle riddle
15. gnome tome
16. bonnet sonnet

## 65.

**WAYS TO TRAVEL:** BUS, TRAIN, JET, BOAT, CAR, SKIS, PLANE
**SEASONS:** SUMMER, FALL, WINTER, SPRING
**FURNITURE:** SOFA, CHEST, TABLE, BED, LAMP, DESK

## 66.

## 67.

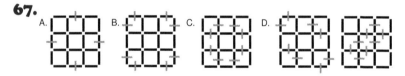

## 68.

1. hand
2. nose
3. liver
4. eye
5. heart
6. brain, ear
7. skin
8. bone
9. thumb
10. mouth

## 69.

France, China, Egypt, Ghana, Brazil, Canada, Japan, India, Russia, Germany, Mexico, Chile

**70.** (Possible answers—not a complete list)

elf, few, floe(s), flow(s), flower, flew, foe(s), for(e), fowl(er)(s), fro, lore, lose(r), low(s), lower(s), ore(s), owe(s), owl(s), roe, role(s), row(s), self, serf, sew, slew, sloe, slow(er), sole, sore, sow(er), swore, woe(s), wolf, wore, worse

**71.**

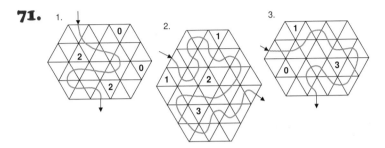

**72.**

| | | | |
|---|---|---|---|
| 1. plain | 9. plane | 17. insane | 25. contain |
| 2. mane | 10. vein | 18. drain | 26. explain |
| 3. lane | 11. main | 19. crane | 27. remain |
| 4. gain | 12. pane | 20. reign | 28. complain |
| 5. cane | 13. slain | 21. grain | 29. wane |
| 6. pain | 14. train | 22. strain | 30. domain |
| 7. brain | 15. rain | 23. vain | |
| 8. chain | 16. stain | 24. rein | |

**73.**

3, 8, 7, 4

**74.**

Sample solutions:

1. (11 + 1) x (1+1) + (1x1)

2. 22 + (2x2) – (2 – 2/2)

3. 3 x 3 x 3 – 3/3 – 3/3

4. 4 x (4+4) - 4 - 4 + 4/4

5. 5 x 5 x [ (5+5)/5 – 5/5 ]

6. 6 x 6 – (66/6) x 6/6

7. 7 x (7+7)/7 + 77/7

8. (8 + 8 + 8 + 8/8) x 8/8

9. 9 + 9 + 9 – 9/9 – 9/9

## 75.
90, 35

## 76.

| O | G | D | R | A | S | N |
|---|---|---|---|---|---|---|
| N | A | R | S | D | O | G |
| S | D | G | A | N | R | O |
| A | S | O | N | R | G | D |
| G | O | N | D | S | A | R |
| D | R | A | G | O | N | S |
| R | N | S | O | G | D | A |

## 77.
**A.** ( + - + ) ( + + ÷ )       **B.** ( + - + + ) ( + ÷ x + )

## 78.
**PLANETS:** MERCURY, VENUS, JUPITER, SATURN, URANUS, NEPTUNE
**TOOLS:** HAMMER, WRENCH, PLIERS, SAW
**NUMBERS:** SIX, ONE, TWO, NINE, TEN

## 79.
Anne—amusement park in IL; Ross—museum in GA; Maria—camping in CO; Scott—zoo in CA

## 80.
8, 3, 7, 5, 4

## 81.

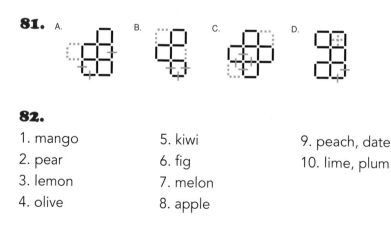

A.   B.   C.   D.

## 82.
1. mango
2. pear
3. lemon
4. olive
5. kiwi
6. fig
7. melon
8. apple
9. peach, date
10. lime, plum

## 83.
19, 32

## 84.
**A.** Fill the 7-cup. Fill the 3-cup from the 7-cup. Empty the 3-cup. Fill the 3-cup from the 7-cup again. You have exactly 1 cup left in the 7-cup.

**B.** Fill the 3-cup. Pour its contents into the 7-cup. Repeat. Repeat again. You now have exactly 2 cups left in the 3-cup.

**C.** Fill the 7-cup. Fill the 3-cup from the 7-cup. Empty the 3 cup. Fill the 3-cup from the 7-cup again. Empty the 3-cup. Pour the 1 cup from the 7-cup into the 3-cup. Fill the 7-cup. Fill the 3-cup from the 7-cup. Exactly 5 cups remain in the 7-cup.

## 85.

| A | T | O | G | E | T | C | I |
|---|---|---|---|---|---|---|---|
| G | T | C | T | A | I | E | O |
| O | E | A | C | I | G | T | T |
| I | C | T | O | T | E | G | A |
| T | I | T | E | C | O | A | G |
| C | O | G | I | T | A | T | E |
| T | G | E | A | O | T | I | C |
| E | A | I | T | G | C | O | T |

## 86.
**WRITING TOOLS:** CRAYON, QUILL, MARKER, PEN, COMPUTER
**FRUITS:** MELON, APPLE, ORANGE, GRAPE, LEMON, PEAR
**BODY PARTS:** HEAD, FOOT, SKIN, CHEST, ANKLE

## 87.

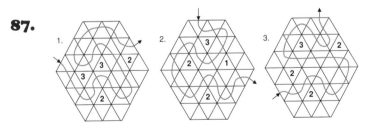

## 88.
**A.** ( x - ÷ + ) ( + - x - )          **B.** ( + ÷ - x ) ( - - - x )

## 89.
5, 9, 2, 4, 7, 3

## 90.
Sample solutions:

1. $(11 - 1) \times (1+1+1) \times 1$
2. $22 + (2 \times 2 \times 2) \times 2/2$
3. $33 - 3/3 - (3+3)/3$
4. $4 + (4 \times 4) + (44 - 4)/4$
5. $(5 \times 5) + 5 - 5 + (5 \times 5/5)$
6. $(6 \times 6) - (6 \times 6/6) + 6 - 6$
7. $7+7+7+7 + (7+7)/7$
8. $8+8+8+8 - (8+8)/8$
9. $9+9+9 + (9+9+9)/9$

## 91.
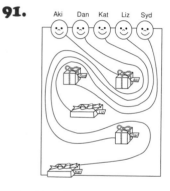

## 92.

| T | G | L | R | E | A | U | H |
|---|---|---|---|---|---|---|---|
| A | E | H | U | G | L | R | T |
| U | L | R | T | A | E | H | G |
| L | A | U | G | H | T | E | R |
| G | T | E | H | R | U | A | L |
| H | R | A | E | T | G | L | U |
| E | H | G | L | U | R | T | A |
| R | U | T | A | L | H | G | E |

## 93.
24

## 94.

1. Spain
2. Canada
3. Peru
4. Turkey
5. Iceland
6. India
7. Nepal
8. Ghana
9. Cuba
10. China

## 95.
**A.** ( x ÷ + - )    **B.** ( x - ÷ + ) ( + + - - ) (- x + - ) ( - ÷ + - ) (÷ + + ÷ )

## 96.
1. night
2. right
3. write
4. kite
5. sight
6. fright
7. bite
8. white
9. tight
10. fight
11. might
12. height
13. sprite
14. knight
15. light
16. bright
17. flight
18. slight
19. unite
20. polite
21. ignite
22. spite
23. rite
24. site
25. mite
26. delight
27. recite
28. dynamite
29. quite
30. trite

## 97.
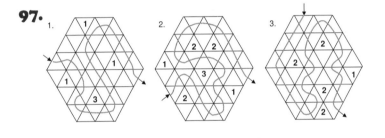

## 98.
Sample solutions:
1. (11 + 1) x (1+1+1) x 1
2. (2 x 2 x 2 x 2 x 2) + 2 + 2
3. (3 x 3) x (3+3+3+3)/3
4. (4 x 4) + (4 x 4) + 4 + 4 - 4
5. (5 x 5) + 55/5 + 5 - 5
6. (6 x 6) x [(6 + 6)/6 – 6/6]
7. 7 + 7 + 7 + 7 + 7 + 7/7
8. 8/(8 + 8) x 8 x (8 + 8/8)
9. 9 + 9 + 9 + 9 + (9-9) x 9

## 99.
8, 3, 9, 5, 6

## 100.
Possible solutions:
**4-letter words**: milk, else, noon, swim, arts
**Vegetables or fruits**: mango, eggplant, nectarine, squash, apple
**Verbs**: make, eat, notice, sing, anticipate

**Bodies of water**: Mississippi River, Erie Canal, Nile River, Sargasso Sea, Amazon River
**Birds:** macaw, emu, nightingale, swan, auk
**Animals (not birds):** mink, elephant, newt, skunk, alpaca
**Body parts**: muscle, ear, nose, stomach, ankle
**Flowers or trees**: marigold, elm, narcissus, sycamore, aster
**Countries**: Mexico, Egypt, Nepal, Spain, Australia
**Things in the solar system**: Mercury, Earth, Neptune, sun, asteroid

Thanks for solving!